This Dandy Annual belongs to...

SUPER-_____

BRIGHTY

THE Dandy

COW PIE

EDITOR-IN-CHIEF — Alexandria Turner
EDITOR — John Anderson
PRODUCTION EDITOR — Michelle O'Donnell
CONTENT EDITOR — Claire Bartlett
CONTENT PRODUCER — Grace Balfour-Harle
DESIGN EDITOR — Leon Strachan
DESIGNER — Mark McIlmail

CONTRIBUTORS

Nigel Auchterlounie
Nigel Parkinson
Shannon Gallant
Laura Howell
Wayne Thompson
The Sharp Bros.

Ned Hartley
Andy Fanton
Danny Pearson
Iain McLaughlin
Hunt Emerson
Mike Donaldson

Shannon Gallant
Lew Stringer
Nick Brennan
Steve Bright
Gary Boller
Mychailo Kazybrid

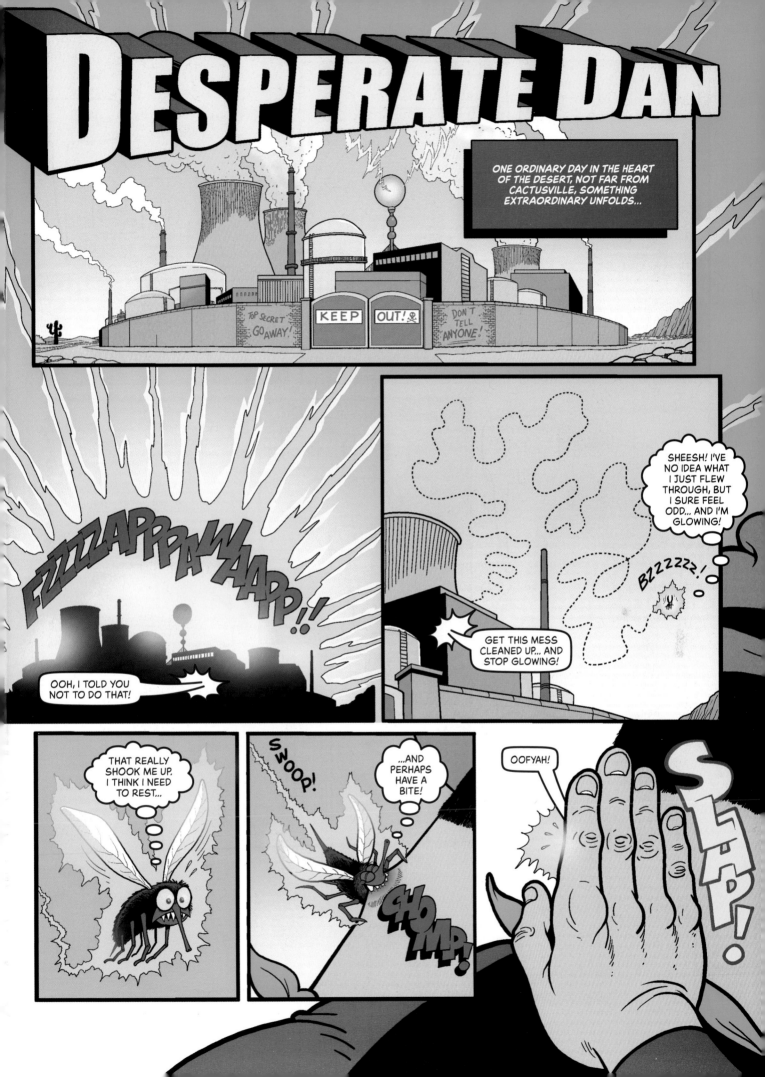

THE JOCKS AND THE GEORDIES

AND STAY OUT!

WAAH!

NICE ONE, DAD. NOW WHAT?

FELIX THE GIANT WOULDN'T GIVE UP SO EASILY, BERYL. HELP US GET IN THERE.

YOU'RE ASKING *ME* FOR HELP?!

FINE, BUT YOU HAVE TO DO MY HOMEWORK FOR A WHOLE YEAR!

DEAL.

SO...

FIRST, WE NEED TO SNEAK IN HERE AND BORROW A COUPLE OF DISGUISES.

TipToe!

I THINK THIS MIGHT BE FELIX THE GIANT'S TRAILER.

TRY AND FIND A DISGUISE THAT MAKES YOU LOOK LIKE A MEAN, TOUGH WRESTLER. I'LL BE YOUR MANAGER.

W.C.

THERE, NOW WE CAN SNEAK IN THROUGH THE BACKSTAGE DOOR AS PART OF THE SHOW.

FLUSH!

WHAT WAS THAT?!

WHAT ARE YOU DOING IN HERE?!

GULP! IT'S FELIX THE GIANT!

QUICK! OUT THE WINDOW!

GRAAR!

HELP ME! BEFORE HE EATS ME FOR DINNER!

IT SOUNDS LIKE HE'S *WRESTLING* WITH A FEW EMOTIONS.

PERFORMERS' ENTRANCE

OUT OF THE WAY! MY GUY IS ON NEXT!

HUH? HE DOESN'T LOOK LIKE MUCH OF A WRESTLER TO ME.

CHARMING.

WELCOME TO THE FIRST, AND MOST PROBABLY LAST, ANNUAL DANDYTOWN'S GOT TALENT SHOW! I'M YOUR HOST, KORKY THE CAT!

OUR JUDGES FOR THE EVENING WILL BE TEACHERS FROM GREYTOWERS SCHOOL.

MR CREEP, THE HEAD AND MR PIGG.

THIS PERSON IS NOT FROM MY SCHOOL!

HAS ANYONE GOT ANY BROWN SAUCE?

WE SCOURED THE ENTIRE TOWN TO BRING YOU ITS GREATEST TALENTS, FOUND NONE AND DECIDED TO LET ANYONE IN!

WHAT ABOUT THE SAUCE?

WITHOUT FURTHER ADO, LET'S HAVE THE FIRST CONTESTANT - KATE.

AND WHAT'S YOUR TALENT?

I LOOK THROUGH KEYHOLES WHICH OFTEN LEADS TO UNLIKELY ADVENTURES,

IS LOOKING THROUGH ANYTHING A TALENT?

ANY BARBECUE SAUCE? NO?

A DOOR IS BROUGHT ONSTAGE...

I AM NOW LOOKING THROUGH THE KEYHOLE,

I SEE...

...NOTHING MUCH. JUST A BIT OF THAT CURTAIN OVER THERE,

GULP! AMAZING! JUDGES, WHAT ARE YOUR THOUGHTS?!

IS THIS HAPPENING?

WONDERFUL! EXCELLENT! THRILLING! ARE ALL WORDS I *WON'T* BE USING!

THE CRUST WAS A BIT DRY WITHOUT ANY SAUCE, TO BE HONEST.

KORKY HAS A MOMENT TO HIMSELF...

CALM DOWN, KORKY! REMEMBER, YOU'RE A CAT AND CATS ARE CHILL. IT'LL BE FINE... AND SO WHAT IF IT'S NOT?

AAARGH

KEEP IT TOGETHER, KORKS! DON'T LET THEM KNOW YOU'RE FREAKING OUT HERE!

ER... WE CAN HEAR YOU.

HA-HA! OF COURSE, YOU CAN! BECAUSE THAT WAS A JOKE, ER... ANYWAY, TIME FOR THE NEXT ACT. WHICH COULDN'T BE WORSE.

FIND OUT LATER WHAT THE NEXT 'TALENTED' ACT IS!

GEORGE vs DRAGON

ROAAAR!

EEK!

WAAH! FEROCIOUS DRAGON!

GRAAARRGH!

I KNEW IT! THAT INFERNAL DRAGON HAS FINALLY GONE *FERAL!*

TIME TO USE *THE WRATHLANCE OF WOEBEGONE* AND VANQUISH THE BEAST!

CRACKLE!

FANTON

HAVE AT YE, YOU FOUL AND WRETCHED BEAST!

OOH!

ZOOM!

HUH? WHAT ARE YOU DOING?

GRAB!

I'VE HAD SOMETHING STUCK IN MY TEETH ALL MORNING! THIS SHOULD HELP GET IT OUT!

STOP THAT!

HMPH! I COULD NOT BE ANY MORE HUMILIATED RIGHT NOW!

WHEE!

SPLUT!

OOFYAH!

CHEERS! THAT BIT OF PINEAPPLE WAS MAKING ME REALLY GRUMPY!

I HATE YOU, DRAGON! AND THAT'S *THE TOOTH!*

DANDYTOWN SCOUTS!

George · Harry · Noah · Olivia · Emily · Meera

NEVER PREPARED!

MEERA IS ARRIVING AT THE DANDYTOWN COMMUNITY HALL...

DANDYTOWN COMMUNITY HALL

TODAY WILL BE DIFFERENT. I CAN FEEL IT!

TODAY IS *ABSOLUTELY* THE DAY ONE OF THEM EARNS A SCOUT BADGE!

SURELY!

GNNNNNNNNNG!

IT'S *PUSH* TO OPEN, REMEMBER, GEORGE?

WAAARRGH!

LET'S SEE IF EVERYBODY'S HERE. JUST SAY, 'PRESENT' IF YOU'RE HERE.

WHAT DO WE SAY IF WE'RE NOT HERE?

SAY, 'ABSENT'.

HOW DOES *THAT* WORK?

OLIVIA, MY BELOVED BIG SISTER, AND ME ARE BOTH HERE.

I CAN SPEAK FOR MYSELF, HARRY!

OKAY, EVERYBODY'S HERE - AND TONIGHT WE ALL START... GETTING A BADGE.

YOU MEAN IT? YOU *REALLY* MEAN IT? WE'RE GOING TO GET AN ACTUAL, REAL BADGE AT LAST?

WELL, THAT'S THE IDEA.

IT'S JUST THAT I'VE ALWAYS WANTED A BADGE - AND WE'RE THE ONLY SCOUT GROUP IN DANDYTOWN WHO DON'T HAVE *ANY*!

DREADLOCK HOLMES

COME ON, KIDS, WE'LL MISS THE TRAIN!

I'M HUNGRY!

WILL SNITCH BE ALLOWED ON THE TRAIN?

OF COURSE, SNITCH CAN COME ON THE TRAIN!

WHY COULDN'T WE HAVE GONE BY PLANE? I COULD BE WATCHING A MOVIE ON THE SMALLEST SCREEN EVER RIGHT NOW!

IT WAS EITHER THIS OR BE STUCK IN A CAR WITH YOUR BROTHER AND A DOG FOR TEN HOURS. WHICH WOULD YOU PREFER?

GULP! NOTHING IS WORSE THAN THAT! I'LL BE GOOD!

HEY! THAT'S NOT NICE!

THIS IS ONE OF THE MOST BEAUTIFUL TRAIN JOURNEYS IN THE WORLD! IT WAS FEATURED IN 'GOING LOCOMOTIVE' MAGAZINE!

GOING LOCOMOTIVE MAGAZINE

ER... MUM? USING MY DETECTIVE SKILLS, I CAN DEDUCE THAT YOUR MAGAZINE IS A BIT OUT OF DATE!

UMM... IT IS IN NEED OF A MAKEOVER, ISN'T IT?

I CAN DEDUCE THAT THIS TRAIN WAS MADE IN 1978 IN SCOTLAND.

THAT'S CLEVER! DID YOU WORK IT OUT FROM THE MAKE AND MODEL OF THE TRAIN, ALONG WITH CLUES ABOUT THE MATERIALS USED?

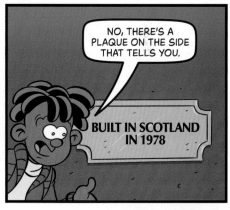

NO, THERE'S A PLAQUE ON THE SIDE THAT TELLS YOU.

BUILT IN SCOTLAND IN 1978

I CAN ALSO DEDUCE THAT THIS TRAIN NEEDS A WASH!

THE 10:30 FROM DANDYTOWN IS LEAVING NOW! ALL ABOARD!

AND THE GUARD! I DON'T REALLY KNOW YOU, BUT THAT DOESN'T MEAN ANYTHING!

WHAT ARE YOU SUGGESTING, KID?

I CAN REVEAL THAT IT WAS...

...I HAVE ABSOLUTELY NO IDEA.

I DON'T KNOW WHICH ONE OF YOU DID THIS.

WAIT A MINUTE... MAYBE ONE OF YOU DIDN'T DO THIS.

YOU HAVE KETCHUP ON YOUR SLEEVE!

YOU HAVE CRUMBS ON YOUR TOP!

YOU HAVE LETTUCE IN YOUR MOUTH!

AND YOU HAVE A PICKLE IN YOUR FUR!

I REALLY SHOULD'VE NOTICED THAT.

YOU ALL ATE PART OF MY BURGER!

SORRY, SHERMAN! I GUESS WE WERE ALL REALLY HUNGRY!

LET'S GO TO THE BUFFET CAR AND GET YOU A REPLACEMENT.

OKAY, BUT BEING A DETECTIVE IS HUNGRY WORK. I'M GOING TO NEED CHIPS AND A DRINK AS WELL!

AND REMEMBER, MUM, IT'S DREADLOCK, NOT SHERMAN!

DANDYTOWN'S GOT T★LENT!

WELCOME BACK TO DANDYTOWN'S GOT TALENT! IT'S TIME FOR OUR NEXT CONTESTANT - DANDYTOWN'S VERY OWN FOOTBALL STAR, OWEN GOAL!

AND WHAT WILL YOU BE DOING FOR US TODAY?

TONIGHT, KORKY, I'LL BE SINGING 'MY HEART WILL GO ON' BY CELINE DION.

WHAT?!

KIDDING! I'LL BE DOING FOOTBALL TRICKS!

HAS ANYONE GOT ANY CREAM FOR THIS BANOFFEE PIE?

IT'S GOT CREAM ON IT.

YES, BUT IT'S WHIPPED CREAM, NOT POURING.

I WILL NOW DO TEN THOUSAND KEEPY-UPPIES!

URRGH! THIS IS GOING TO TAKE AGES!

IT DOESN'T TAKE AGES...

ONE...

Bosh!

Bosh!

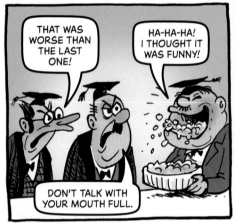

THAT WAS WORSE THAN THE LAST ONE!

HA-HA-HA! I THOUGHT IT WAS FUNNY!

DON'T TALK WITH YOUR MOUTH FULL.

SORRY ABOUT THAT! I WAS WARMING UP. THIS TIME WILL BE BETTER!

SPLAT!

HA-HA-HA! NOW THAT'S ENTERTAINMENT!

OFF! GET OFF! IT'S TIME FOR THE NEXT CONTESTANT!

BUT I'M JUST WARMING UP!

FIND OUT LATER WHO'S NEXT!

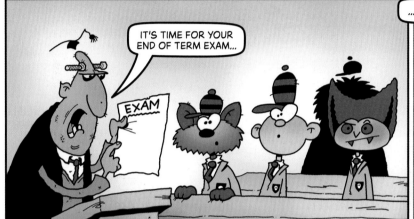

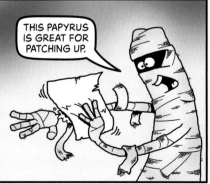

TAKE THESE TO THE OFFICIAL EXAM MARKER.

IT'LL TAKE AGES TO MARK THIS LOT.

EXAM MARKER

CREAK!

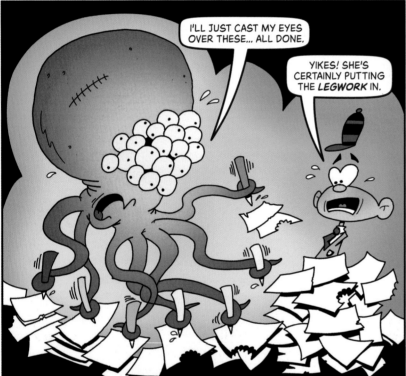

I'LL JUST CAST MY EYES OVER THESE... ALL DONE.

YIKES! SHE'S CERTAINLY PUTTING THE *LEGWORK* IN.

SO...

YOU ALL DID VERY WELL...

RESULTS

...EXCEPT POTTER, HE GOT 98%

?!

BLIMEY! IF MY SCORE'S NO GOOD, WHAT DID THEY ALL GET?

ZERO. EXACTLY WHAT WE EXPECT FROM STRANGE HILL PUPILS.

RESULTS
WOLFIE 0%
VAMPIRA 0%
POTTER 98%
EGOR 0%
MUMMY 0%

MOST OF YOU DID WELL, SO WE'LL STILL GO TO THE FAIR...

...BUT AS PUNISHMENT FOR BEING SO RUBBISH, POTTER WILL RECORD OUR TRIP ON THE SCHOOL TABLET.

THAT'S NOT SO BAD...

...I LIKE PLAYING WITH TECH!

HERE YOU ARE, DON'T BREAK IT.

YIKES! IT'S A STONE TABLET!

YOU'LL NEED THESE, TOO.

OOF.

SOON...

TAP! TAP!

ALL ABOARD!

DON'T FORGET - THE HEAD'S COMING ALONG, AND SHE'LL WANT YOU ALL ON YOUR WORST BEHAVIOUR.

WHAT LUCK! PERFECT WEATHER FOR A PICNIC.

CLATTER!

SPLASH!

I DON'T BELIEVE IT...

...IT'S A NORMAL FAIR.

OF COURSE, AND WE ALWAYS GET V.I.P. TREATMENT HERE.

WHAT A BRILLIANT TREAT!

JUST THROUGH HERE.

CLANG!

HUH?

CHAMBER of HORRORS

ROLL UP! ROLL UP! SEE THE MOST 'ORRIBLE THINGS YOU'VE EVER SEEN!

WE'LL BE DRENCHING YOU WITH ICE-COLD SLIME SOON.

LOVELY!

URRGH! MONSTERS!

URRGH! NORMAL PEOPLE!

SIGH! I SHOULD HAVE KNOWN.

DANGER KEEP CLEAR

THE END

DANDYTOWN'S GOT T★LENT!

WELCOME BACK TO DANDYTOWN'S GOT TALENT! IT'S TIME FOR OUR NEXT CONTESTANT - BERYL THE PERIL!

AND WHAT WILL YOU BE DOING FOR US TODAY, BERYL?

TONIGHT, KORKY, I'LL BE PUTTING MYSELF IN PERIL BY JUGGLING CHAINSAWS.

NO, YOU WON'T, YOUNG LADY! THAT'S FAR TOO DANGEROUS!

URRGH! DAD! YOU'RE SO EMBARRASSING!

OKAY, WHAT IF I JUGGLE...

...PIES?

WHAT?!

YOU'LL GET THEM BACK, MAYBE OR MAYBE NOT SMASHED!

NO!

UNHAND THOSE PIES!

HEY, DON'T GET SO CLOSE!

MR PIGG GETS TOO CLOSE...

ARRGH...

SCOOP

BERYL! UNHAND THAT TEACHER!

DAD GETS TOO CLOSE...

ARGH!

ARRG.

AS DOES KORKY...

STOP JUGGLING US!

I DON'T KNOW HOW TO STOP! I SUPPOSE I JUST...

...STOP.

CRASH!

BET I WIN!

THE JOCKS AND THE GEORDIES

JUST LOOK AT THAT, LADS, DID YE EVER THINK YOU'D SEE THE LIKE?

IT'S OUR BIG CHANCE TO BE ON TV, TO MAKE OUR PARENTS AND SCOTLAND PROUD.

SCHOOL CHALLENGE ON icu2

SUNDAYS AFTER TEA

AYE,

IT'LL BE BRAW.

THE ONLY WAY YOU'LL BE ON TELLY IS ON 'BRITAIN'S LEAST WANTED'.

YOU WON'T GET A SINGLE QUESTION RIGHT.

YOU WON'T EVEN GET *YOUR OWN NAMES* RIGHT.

WE'LL SEE ABOUT THAT!

AYE, WE'LL WIN THIS TV SHOW FOR SURE.

AND THEN YOU'LL WAKE UP AND GET TRASHED ON THE REAL SHOW, MAN.

AND WHEN WE WIN, WE'LL WALK AWAY WITH THAT *BIG CASH PRIZE.*

BIG?

CASH?

PRIZE?

MY THREE FAVOURITE WORDS.

icu

RIGHT, LADS, CHANGE OF PLAN, THEY AREN'T GOING TO WIN THAT PRIZE, WE ARE.

HOW CAN WE DO THAT? THEY'LL NEVER LET US IN.

MAIN GATE CHECK POINT

WE'RE ANT AND DEC.

AND SO ARE WE, MAN.

AND I'M CHERYL COLE.

THE "LIST"

THEY'RE ON SO MANY PROGRAMMES I KNEW THERE HAD TO BE MORE THAN JUST TWO OF THEM.

CHERYL LOOKS YOUNGER THAN SHE DOES ON TELLY, MIND.

IT'S NORMAN STREET SCHOOL. THEY MUST BE ON AGAINST THE JOCKS.

WHAT? THE NORMAL NORMANS? THE MOST BORING SCHOOL IN TOON?

EXIT

SIT DOWN, NORMANS.

WE WILL, NORMA.

AFTER YOU, NORMAN.

NO, YOU FIRST, NORMAN.

SQUEAL!

I WONDER WHO LEFT THOSE PRANK SPRING-CHAIRS THERE?

IT IS A MYSTERY, HA-HA!

CAN'T LET THE EMPTY SEATS GO TO WASTE, MAN.

AND TALKING OF WASTE, THERE'S THEM WASTE OF SPACE JOCKS.

HOW DID YOU GET HERE?

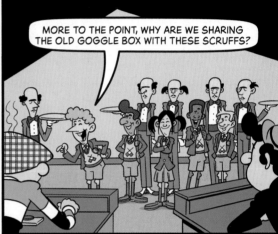

MORE TO THE POINT, WHY ARE WE SHARING THE OLD GOGGLE BOX WITH THESE SCRUFFS?

OH NO, IT'S DANDYTOWN ACADEMY. WE HATE THEM!

WE ONLY HAD YOU INVITED ON THE BALLY OLD SHOW BECAUSE YOU'D BE SO EASY TO BEAT. DADDY OWNS THE NETWORK, YOU KNOW.

IS THAT RIGHT? WE'LL GET TO THE GEORDIES AFTER WE SEE OFF THAT BUNCH.

I'VE GOT A PLAN TO CLEAN THEM OUT.

CRIKEY!

ONE SAYS!

THIS NEVER HAPPENS AT POSHTON ABBEY!

IT WAS SUPPOSED TO BE THOSE TWITS THAT STARTED SLIDING.

OH NO, SIR. IT IS OUR JOB - AND OUR HONOUR, SO THEY TELL US - TO PUT OURSELVES IN HARM'S WAY TO PROTECT THE YOUNG MASTERS.

GASP!

WHAT NOW?

SHUCKS! THIS SURE AIN'T CACTUSVILLE'S LUCKY DAY, IS IT?

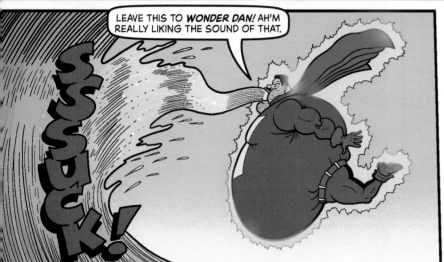

LEAVE THIS TO *WONDER DAN!* AH'M REALLY LIKING THE SOUND OF THAT.

SSSDUCK!

SCREEEEEAM

WHAT NOW?

HERE WE GO AGAIN - ANOTHER JOB FOR *WONDER DAN!*

ALL PART OF THE SERVICE!

SCOOSH!

HSSSS!

YAY! *WONDER DAN* SAVES THE DAY... AGAIN!

THREE TIMES ALREADY!

OH NO! THIS IS A DISASTER!

WHY, THAT'S AUNT AGGIE'S VOICE I DETECT WITH MA SUPER-HEARING - SOMETHING IS TERRIBLY WRONG!

MORE SUPER ADVENTURES WITH WONDER DAN TO COME, READERS...

GEORGE vs DRAGON

OFFICER BOBBY

KID COPS

SGT. NICK

BOYS, TIDY UP YOUR TOYS. IT'S ALMOST TIME FOR BED!

TOYS?

TOYS?

WE'LL HAVE YOU KNOW, MRS MUM, THIS IS A CRIME SCENE!

NOTHING SHOULD BE DISTURBED UNTIL WE SOLVE THIS CRIME!

HA-HA! YOU BOYS AND YOUR IMAGINATION! ALL RIGHT, FIVE MORE MINUTES!

MR BEAR, FOR LEGAL REASONS, THIS INTERVIEW IS BEING RECORDED...

...ON A SHEET OF PAPER WITH OUR BEST CRAYONS!

INTERVOOW WIV TEDDY BEAR

MR BEAR, WHERE WERE YOU ON MONDAY EVENING?

WHICH IS TODAY, ABOUT HALF AN HOUR AGO.

EXERCISING YOUR RIGHT TO REMAIN SILENT, EH?

ER... I CAN'T SPELL ALL THAT, SO I'LL JUST PUT 'BEAR SAID NUFFINK'!

WE CAN'T FINISH OUR TOY POLICE STATION BECAUSE SOME BUILDING BLOCKS HAVE VANISHED!

YOU WERE THE ONLY PERSON IN THE AREA WHEN WE FORGOT WHERE WE PUT THEM. AHEM, I MEAN... WHEN THE BRICKS WENT MISSING!

HAVE YOU CHECKED HIS POCKETS, OFFICER BOBBY?

NO POCKETS, SERGEANT NICK! IT'S A MYSTERY INDEED!

WE'LL SEE IF YOU'RE STILL SMILING AFTER A NIGHT IN THE CELLS, MR BEAR!

WE COULDN'T BUILD THE CELLS BECAUSE WE RAN OUT OF BRICKS, SARGE!

OUCH!

SOUNDS LIKE DAD!

OW! OW! OW!

YAY! DAD'S FOUND THE BRICKS AND SOLVED THE MYSTERY!

SEEMS YOU'RE FREE TO GO, MR BEAR! WELL? DON'T JUST SIT THERE OR WE'LL ARREST YOU FOR LOITERING!

DREADLOCK HOLMES

HEY, SNITCH!

LOOK AT THIS! THERE'S A NEW WORD GAME AND I BET I'M GOING TO BE REALLY GOOD AT IT!

I KNOW YOU'RE A DOG, BUT I NEED TO SHOW OFF TO SOMEONE.

IT'S BECAUSE I'M SO BRILLIANT AT DEDUCTIVE REASONING!

THERE ARE PERKS TO BEING THE WORLD'S GREATEST DETECTIVE, YOU KNOW!

MAYBE IT'S THIS WORD.

OR, THIS.

SO IT MUST BE...

BEEP!

BEEP!

BEEP!

ARRGH! ONE MORE WRONG ANSWER AND I LOSE THE GAME!

THAT CAN'T HAPPEN.

WOOF! WOOF!

NOT NOW, SNITCH! THIS IS IMPORTANT?! I'LL ASK MUM IF SHE'S GOT IT.

MUM! DID YOU SOLVE THE WORD GAME TODAY?! I NEED TO KNOW!

YES, SHERMAN. IT WAS A TRICKY ONE.

CAN YOU GIVE ME A CLUE? PLEEEEEEEEEASE? I'LL EVEN OVERLOOK THE FACT YOU CALLED ME SHERMAN.

HA-HA! OKAY, HERE'S A CLUE, IT'S SOMETHING THAT IS CLOSE TO HOME FOR YOU.

DREADLOCK HAS TOO MANY LETTERS.

SO HAS DETECTIVE!

THE WORD TODAY ISN'T 'MARSHA', IS IT?

LEAVE ME ALONE, SHERMAN, YOU'RE BEING WEIRD AGAIN.

ARRGH! MY PHONE! IT'S GONE! AND IT'S DREADLOCK TO YOU!

IT'S A *MYSTERY!* THE MYSTERY OF THE MISSING PHONE!

I MEAN, IT'S NOT EXACTLY A MAJOR CRIME, BUT IT'S STILL A MYSTERY FOR ME TO INVESTIGATE.

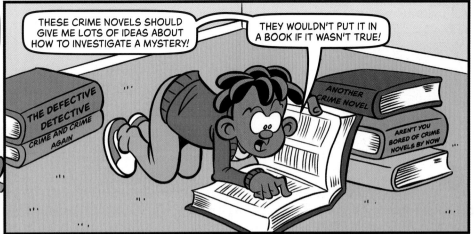

THESE CRIME NOVELS SHOULD GIVE ME LOTS OF IDEAS ABOUT HOW TO INVESTIGATE A MYSTERY!

THEY WOULDN'T PUT IT IN A BOOK IF IT WASN'T TRUE!

THE DEFECTIVE DETECTIVE

CRIME AND CRIME AGAIN

ANOTHER CRIME NOVEL

AREN'T YOU BORED OF CRIME NOVELS BY NOW

I WISH YOU'D PUT THIS MUCH EFFORT INTO YOUR HOMEWORK!

IT'S AN IMPORTANT CASE, CHIEF! THIS TIME IT'S PERSONAL!

THE DEFECTIVE DETECTIVE

CRIME AND CRIME AGAIN

FIRST, I NEED TO SECURE THE CRIME SCENE! I'LL USE THIS CRIME SCENE TAPE TO KEEP PEOPLE AWAY.

ERK! IT'S A BIT STICKY!

WAAH! I'M WRAPPED UP LIKE A MUMMY! *I NEED MY MUMMY!*

WHAT ARE YOU DOING NOW?

I'M SOLVING CRIMES, CHIEF!

I NEED A LIST OF SUSPECTS!

DON'T KNOW

NO IDEA

HAVEN'T A CLUE

ABSOLUTELY STUMPED

HMM... THIS ISN'T VERY HELPFUL.

I NEED EVIDENCE! I'LL USE THIS FLOUR TO DUST FOR FINGERPRINTS.

UMM... I CAN'T SEE MY OWN FINGERS, LET ALONE ANYONE ELSE'S FINGERPRINTS!

RIGHT, THAT'S IT! YOU'VE MADE ENOUGH MESS! OUT OF THE KITCHEN, YOU!

YOU CAN'T TAKE ME OFF THIS CASE, CHIEF!

HAVE YOU FINISHED MAKING A MASSIVE MESS, SHERMAN?

GRR! MARSHA, I HAVEN'T EVEN *STARTED* MAKING A MESS!

DID YOU STEAL MY PHONE?

IF YOU'VE LOST YOUR PHONE, WHY DON'T YOU JUST CALL IT? I THOUGHT YOU WERE SUPPOSED TO BE CLEVER!

I *AM* CLEVER. I WOULD'VE THOUGHT OF THAT SOONER OR LATER.

THAT'S MY PHONE! BUT WHERE IS IT?

RING! RING! RING!

I TOLD YOU I DIDN'T TAKE IT!

SNITCH!

RING! RING!

AND YOU SOLVED THE WORD PUZZLE? IT WAS *SNITCH* ALL ALONG!

YOU'RE A *DOGGONE* GENIUS, JUST LIKE ME!

SNITCH

WOOF!

DANDYTOWN'S GOT TALENT!

WELCOME BACK TO DANDYTOWN'S GOT TALENT! IT'S TIME FOR OUR NEXT CONTESTANT... BRASSNECK!

WHAT WILL YOU BE DOING FOR US TODAY, BRASSNECK?

I HOPE TO AMAZE YOU ALL WITH MY ACROBATICS!

IS ACROBATICS ANYTHING TO DO WITH FOOD?

NO.

I DON'T LIKE IT, THEN.

YOU TWO LOOK VERY SIMILAR, ARE YOU RELATED?

NO!

MUM WAS WONDERING WHY YOU NEVER SHOWED FOR DINNER LAST SATURDAY.

BECAUSE THERE'S NO POINT WHEN YOU'RE THERE! *YOU* SCOFF ALL THE GRUB!

WHO? ME?!

ER... HELLO?! DID YOU SEE THOSE CARTWHEELS I JUST DID?

YES, CARRY ON.

NOW I SHALL STAND ON MY HANDS!

I JUST NEED TO SWAP THESE, AND...

CLICK

...TA-DA!

GET IT?!

SILENCE!

OKAY, I SHALL NOW DO A 600-TURN BACKFLIP!

BALANCING ON HIS HANDS, BRASSNECK SPINS AT INCREDIBLE SPEED...

I HOPE *THIS* GETS THE JUDGES' ATTENTION!

YOU HAD ALL THE CAKE AT MY BIRTHDAY!

ER, GUYS...

WATCH OUT! I'M OUT OF CONTROL!

IT'S SAFE TO SAY BRASSNECK GOT THE JUDGES' ATTENTION. FIND OUT LATER IF HE WON. (SPOILER - HE DIDN'T!)

SWEETIE VILLE   KANE VILLE   LAYLA VILLE   THE TRIPLETS

MY MUM'S A... SUPER Villain

PARENTS! WE DEMAND NAMES! SWEETIE HAS ONE.

OKAY, YOU CAN BE CERBERUS AFTER THE MYTHICAL MANY-HEADED DOG, YOU CAN BE HYDRA AFTER THE MYTHICAL MANY-HEADED SNAKE, AND YOU CAN BE... TIM.

NOW LEAVE US! WE'RE BUSY WITH AN EVIL PLAN, MWAH-HA-HA!

SWEETIE IS LISTENING IN...

UH-OH! MY PARENTS HAVE ANOTHER EVIL PLAN I NEED TO FOIL!

TIM?! WHAT KIND OF EVIL NAME IS TIM?!

YES! OUR EVIL ROBOT IS FINISHED!

IT'S NOT EVIL YET, IT NEEDS AN EVIL MIND, THAT'S WHERE THIS MIND-SCANNER COMES IN.

IT'S GOING TO COPY YOUR EVILNESS AND UPLOAD IT TO THE ROBOT'S MIND.

I WAS WONDERING WHAT IT DID.

GASP! HOW CAN I STOP THIS?

NOT NOW, GLOPPITY GLOB!

NUMMY NUMS!

NUM NUM NUMS!

WHAT MY FRIEND IS TRYING TO SAY IS, WE'RE HUNGRY, FEED US.

YOU'RE *ALWAYS* HUNGRY!

ALWAYS FEED US!

NUMS?

MEANWHILE, MUM SCANS CERBERUS'S EVIL MIND...

HA-HA! THAT TICKLES!

ZOOP!

BUT...

URRGH! IT'S TAKING AGES TO UPLOAD.

LET'S GO FOR LUNCH.

NOW'S MY CHANCE! IF I SCAN MYSELF, I CAN UPLOAD MY GOODNESS INTO THE ROBOT!

NUMMY NUMS!

SHOO! I'M BUSY!

AND WE'RE HUNGRY FOR NUMS!

OW-OW-OW!

EEK! LET'S TRY ANOTHER ACT!

I'LL SHOW YOU MY MAGIC ACT.

I SHOULD BE ABLE TO PULL A RABBIT FROM THE HAT... IF I CAN FIND IT.

ARRGH! HELP!

I'M PRETTY SURE THE RABBIT'S NOT SUPPOSED TO PULL *YOU* INTO THE HAT.

PAINTING THE SCENERY IS FUN. NOTHING CAN GO WRONG HERE.

WANNA BET?

I THINK YOU BROUGHT THE *HOUSE DOWN.*

YIKES!

THAT MEANS THERE'S ONLY LITTLE *ME* LEFT. NOW I'VE FINISHED THAT TOFFEE, I SHALL NOW SING *20 OR 30* OF MY FAVOURITE SONGS!

DON'T WORRY! I CAN FIX THIS!

OH NO. I'M STANDING ON A...

...TRAPDOOR!

YOU *WERE* STANDING ON IT - NOW YOU'RE PLUMMETING THROUGH IT.

SIGH... I THINK WE'LL JUST DRAW A VEIL OVER THIS PARTICULAR BADGE! *SHOW'S OVER!*

WHOOSH!!

WAAH! I SAID SLOWLY!

CRAB OVERBOARD!

ARRGH! GET IT OFF ME.

NIP!

HOLD STILL, I'LL GET IT OFF FOR YOU.

UH-OH! THEY LOOK A LITTLE *CRABBY*.

NIP!

WAAH! THE CRABS ARE TRYING TO TAKE OVER THE PIER! RUN FOR YOUR LIVES!

I'M THE MANAGER OF THIS PIER, I SUGGEST YOU AND YOUR DAUGHTER LEAVE, NOW!

YAY! ENOUGH OF THIS *PIER PRESSURE*, BACK TO THE ARCADE WE GO.

BUT DAD HAS OTHER IDEAS...

REMIND ME AGAIN WHY WE'RE HERE AND NOT IN THE ARCADE?

WE'RE HERE TO RELAX AND GET AWAY FROM TECHNOLOGY.

BESIDES, YOU HAVE NO MONEY LEFT. SETTLE DOWN AND ENJOY THE BEACH.

HE'S RIGHT. I NEED TO FIND A WAY TO MAKE SOME CASH.

PERFECT. ALL I NEED TO DO IS MAKE A WINNING SAND SCULPTURE.

SAND SCULPTURE COMPETITION 1ˢᵗ PRIZE £50

LATER...

IT'S GOOD...

...BUT IT'S NOT GREAT. MY SANDMAN JUST ISN'T REALISTIC ENOUGH.

DAD MAY BE ABLE TO HELP ME. I NEED TO *SEAS* THIS OPPORTUNITY.

ZZZ

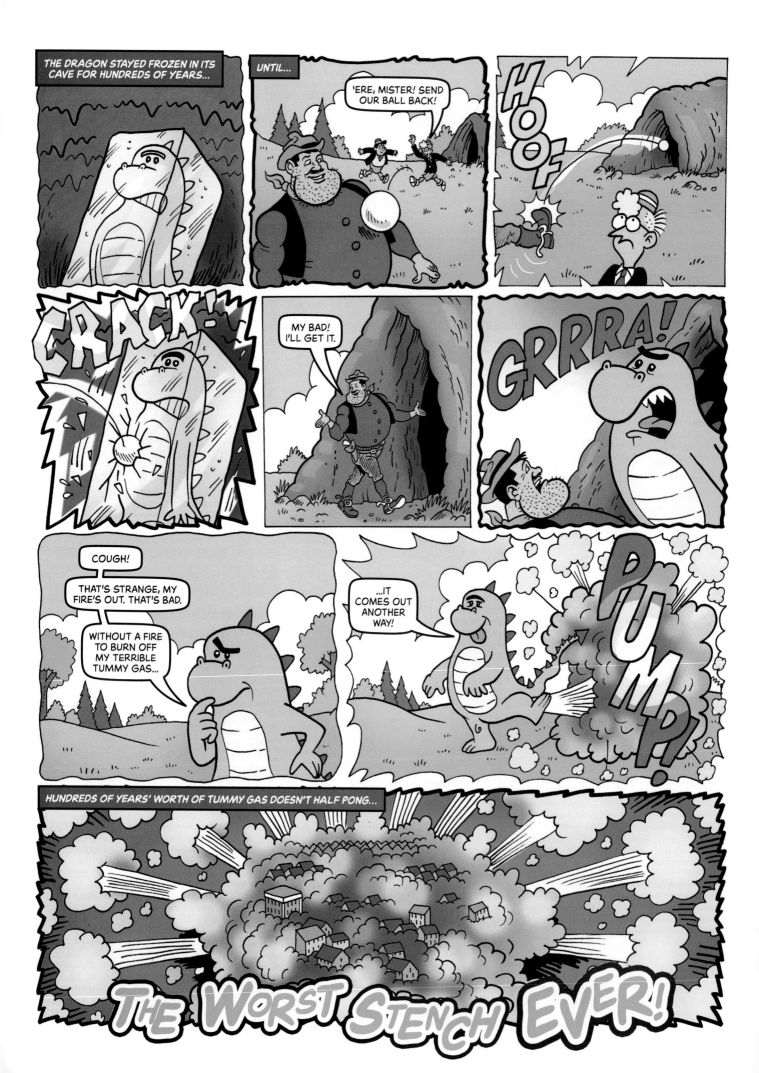

HOW LONG WILL THE JOURNEY TO THE MOON TAKE? DAYS? WEEKS?

WE'RE HERE!

AS THE MIGHTY ROCKET LANDS, IT FIRES PODS OUT ACROSS THE MOON'S SURFACE...

P-TOO! P-TOO! P-TOO! P-TOO!

EACH POD IS A PLASTIC BUBBLE WITH A HOUSE IN IT...

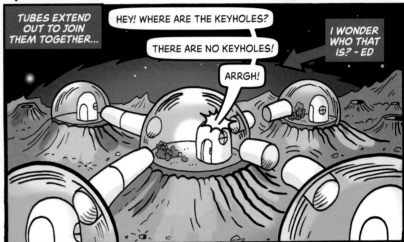

TUBES EXTEND OUT TO JOIN THEM TOGETHER...

HEY! WHERE ARE THE KEYHOLES?

THERE ARE NO KEYHOLES!

ARRGH!

I WONDER WHO THAT IS? - ED

AFTERNOON, NEIGHBOUR.

I'M STILL SURPRISED WE BUILT THE ROCKET AND THESE PODS IN A DAY.

IT SEEMS FAR-FETCHED.

THIS IS A NEW WORLD! A CLEAN, UNSPOILT WILDERNESS.

SLURP!

A CHANCE TO START AGAIN WITHOUT MAKING THE SAME MISTAKES HUMANITY MADE IN THE PAST.

SOUNDS GREAT, LET'S GO FOR IT!

DUMP!

UH-OH! FIND OUT WHAT HAPPENS NEXT IN PART TWO, LATER IN THE ANNUAL.

DANDYTOWN'S GOT T★LENT!

WELCOME BACK TO DANDYTOWN'S GOT TALENT! IT'S TIME FOR OUR NEXT CONTESTANT - SMASHER!

AND WHAT WILL YOU BE DOING FOR US TODAY, SMASHER?

TODAY, KORKY, I'LL BE...

YOU'LL BE DOING NOTHING! GET OFF! NEXT!

WHAT? WHY?!

SO FAR, WE'VE BEEN HIT BY FOOTBALLS, CAKE AND EVEN PEOPLE! AND BRASSNECK CRASHED INTO US.

SO?

SO, YOU'RE SMASHER. WHATEVER YOU DO, SOMETHING WILL GET SMASHED - ON US!

HE'S GOT A POINT.

I'VE NEVER BEEN SO INSULTED IN ALL MY LIFE! I DON'T HAVE TO STAND HERE AND TAKE THIS! GOODBYE!

HUFF!

SMASHER BUMPS INTO THE STAGE BACKDROP...

OW!

OOPS!

BUMP!

UH-OH!

SMASH!

SORRY!

WHAT WAS YOUR TALENT?

I WAS GOING TO DO SOME IMPRESSIONS.

SOMEONE CALLED DENNIS?

WHO? NEVER HEARD OF HIM!

GEORGE vs DRAGON

I DUB THEE... SIR PRISE!

WOW! I WAS NOT EXPECTING THIS!

BAH!

FANTON.

WHY DO I NEVER GET A KNIGHTHOOD? I SHOULD BE HONOURED FOR MY SERVICES TO DRAGON CATCHING!

OF COURSE, IT'D HELP IF I ACTUALLY *CAUGHT* A DRAGON! GRR!

TRA-LA-LAAA!

I KNOW! IF I LEAD THAT DOPEY DRAGON UP TO THE CASTLE, I COULD CATCH HIM RIGHT IN FRONT OF THE KING!

I'D BE UP TO MY EYEBALLS IN KNIGHTHOODS THEN!

SO...

THIS SHOULD TEMPT THE DRAGON ALONG!

DROP!

YE CASTLE

OOH! CAKES! YUMMY!

HERE HE COMES! I HAVE A LITTLE SURPRISE WAITING FOR HIM! HEH-HEH!

YE TRIP WIRE!

CHOMP!

WOO-HOO! MORE CAKE...

...WAAAH!

UH-OH! I MAY NOT HAVE THOUGHT THIS THROUGH!

TRIP!

EGAD! WHO DARES DISTURB THE ROYAL BUSINESS?!

YE THRONE ROOM

SIRES

CRASH!

GRR! WHO TRIPPED A DRAGON INTO MY CASTLE? I'D LIKE A WORD WITH THEM!

AT LEAST GEORGE HAS HIS *KNIGHT HOOD* NOW! CHUCKLE!

GULP! GOTTA HIDE!

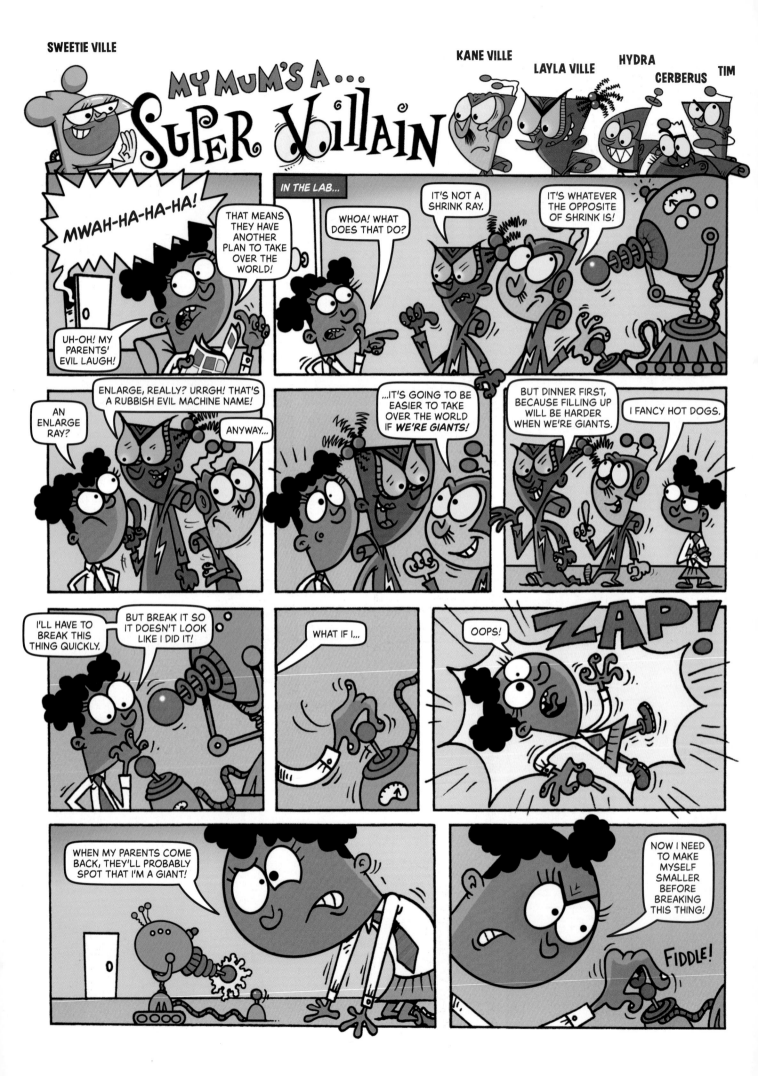

OFFICER BOBBY

KID COPS

SGT. NICK

WE'RE ON PATROL, KEEPING THE STREETS OF DANDYTOWN SAFE 24/7!

OR AT LEAST UNTIL MUM CALLS US IN FOR LUNCH!

SQUEAK! SQUEAK! SQUEAK!

Police

LITTLE LEGS PEDALLING LIKE THE CLAPPERS!

HUR-HUR! I CAN WALK FASTER THAN YOUR STUPID PEDAL CAR!

HEY! RESPECT THE LAW, CITIZEN!

Police

ACTUALLY, THIS IS HARD WORK! IT'S QUICKER IF WE WALK TOO!

OKAY, LET'S POUND THE BEAT WITH OUR FEET!

POLICE

GIMME YOUR APPLE, WIMP!

IT'S THAT BULLY AGAIN!

STOP IN THE NAME OF THE LAW!

GRAB!

HA! MY LONG LEGS CAN EASILY OUTRUN YOU!

I CAN'T KEEP UP!

BAH! HE GOT AWAY!

NO PROBLEM! I'LL DRAW A WANTED POSTER WITH MY BEST CRAYONS!

THERE! TAPED TO A TREE SO EVERYONE CAN SEE IT!

WANTiD MEEN LOOKING BULLY

IT LOOKS NOTHING LIKE HIM! THAT WON'T CATCH HIM!

GUST!

WANTiD MEEN LOOKING BULLY

OOPS! THAT DIDN'T STAY UP LONG!

HUR! THIS APPLE WAS DELICIOUS 'COS IT WAS FREE!

GUST!

EEK! WHAT'S THIS?

WANTiD MEEN LOOKING BULLY

I CAN'T SEE WHERE I'M G...GAH!

TRIP!

WANTiD MEEN LOOKING BULLY

SPLAT!

LEN STRINGER

YAY! MY POSTER CAUGHT HIM AFTER ALL!

JUSTICE IS SERVED! BULLYING LED TO YOUR DOWNFALL!

GROAN!

WANTiD MEEN LOOKING BULLY

DESPERATE DAN

DAN HAS BEEN BITTEN BY A RADIOACTIVE MOSQUITO, GIVING HIM AMAZING SUPERPOWERS, AND A BIT OF A BIG HEAD, IF WE'RE HONEST...

THE COAST IS CLEAR. THIS IS TOO EASY!

UH-OH! DOC WEEKEND-BREAK AND HIS GANG HAVE ROBBED THE BANK! - ED

WHIP!

WHAT IN TARNATION IS HAPPENING?

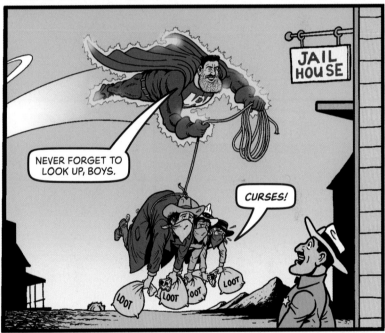

NEVER FORGET TO LOOK UP, BOYS.

CURSES!

LATER...

I CAUGHT THESE RUSTLERS DURING MA LUNCH BREAK, SHERIFF.

WE'RE GONNA NEED US A BIGGER JAILHOUSE AT THIS RATE!

HEY - I'M INNOCENT!

FIGHTIN' CRIME IS EVEN MORE FUN THAN AVERTING NATURAL DISASTERS.

NO CRIMINAL IS A MATCH FOR WONDER DAN!

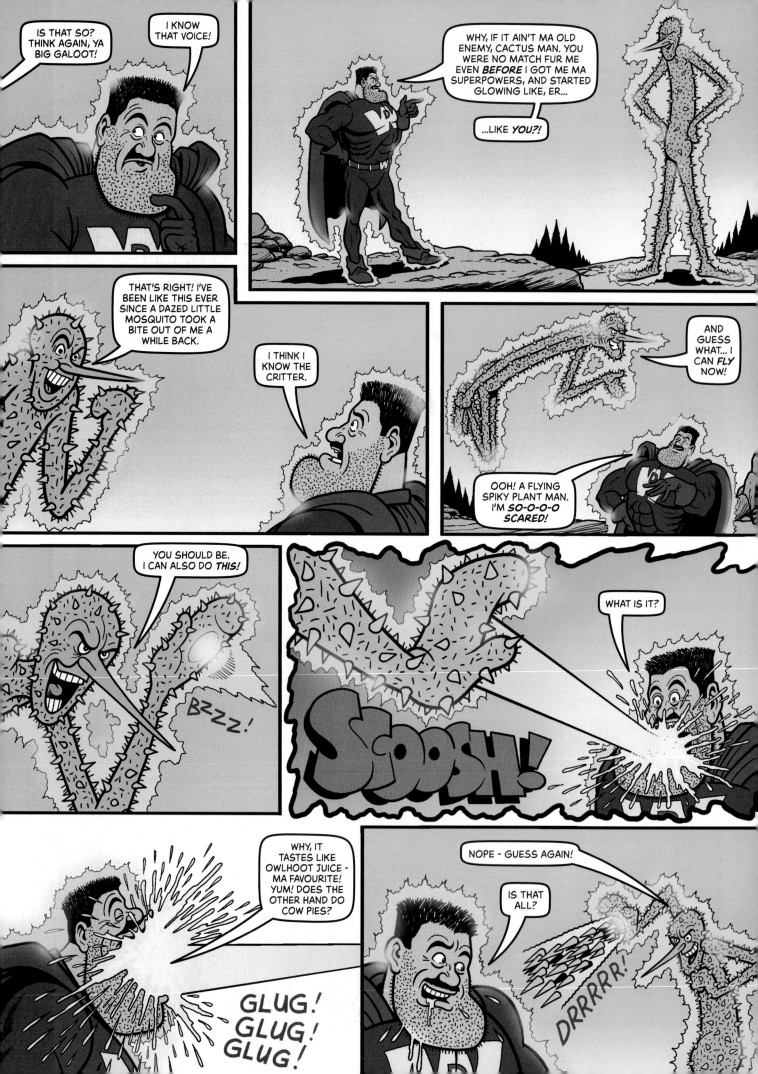

BACK AT THE CABIN...

GRUMBLE! DAD! IT'S STARTED TO RAIN.

CAN YOU HEAR THE HYPNOTIC PATTERING SOUND OF RAINDROPS ON THE ROOF?

NO! I CAN FEEL IT FLOOD THROUGH ONE OF THE MANY HOLES IN THE ROOF!

OH!

WHERE ARE YOU GOING?

GRR! I'M GOING TO GET SOME FRESH AIR.

IN THE RAIN?

SO...

I'M SURE THE PARK OWNER WILL BEAR-LY EVEN NOTICE ME BORROWING THIS, TIME TO SEND DAD PACKING.

BACK AT THE CABIN...

DAD, I THINK THERE'S SOMETHING OUTSIDE!

SOMEONE'S BEEN WATCHING TOO MANY SCARY FILMS.

THERE'S NOTHING OUTSIDE, I'LL SHOW Y...

...ARRGH! A BEAR!

OH NO, HOW TERRIFYING, NOW CAN WE GO HOME?

YES! GET IN THE CAR BEFORE THAT BEAR GETS ITS PAWS ON US.

SECONDS LATER...

LET'S GET OUT OF HERE!

YAY!

ZOOM!

TUT! CITY FOLK, WHAT'S MY STUFFED BEAR DOING OUT HERE?

BACK HOME...

CHECK ALL THE WINDOWS ARE LOCKED, THAT BEAR MIGHT HAVE FOLLOWED US.

I COULDN'T BEAR THE THOUGHT OF STAYING AT THAT PLACE FOR ONE MORE MINUTE! THERE'S NO PLACE LIKE HOME.

THE JOCKS AND THE GEORDIES

THERE'S ONLY ONE THING TO DO ON A HOT DAY LIKE THIS, LADS - HAVE A GAME OF CRICKET.

CRICKET? WHAT A DAFT GAME, WHY DON'T YOU PLAY A PROPER ONE?

AYE... LIKE SHINTY OR CURLING OR CHASING-THE-HAGGIS-ROOND-THE-MOUNTAIN.

I'M PRETTY SURE THAT LAST ONE'S JUST FOR TOURISTS, ECK.

IGNORE THEM, LADS, THEY'RE NOT WORTH WOR TIME, UNLESS WE SAY...

RASSSZZZPPPP!

RIGHT, LADS, NOBODY RASPS AT US AND GETS AWAY WITH IT, WE'LL BEAT THEM AT THEIR OWN GAME.

HOW? WE KNOW NOTHING ABOUT CRICKET.

TRUE... BUT WE KNOW HOW TO CHEAT!

AYE, WE DO THAT.

SO...

REET, LADS, THIS LOOKS LIKE A CANNY PLACE TO SET UP THE WICKET.

AND SET UP THE SMASHIN' TEA WE HAVE - YE CAN'T HAVE CRICKET WITHOUT TEA.

WE'D BETTER MARK OUT THE PITCH.

YOU CALL THAT SETTING UP A PITCH? DON'T YOU KNOW ANYTHING ABOUT CRICKET?

MORE THAN YOU DO.

DO YOU THINK SO? MY BOOK HERE DISAGREES, THIS HAS ALL THE RULES OF CRICKET.

HEAVY
TWO TO LIFT

THE GREAT BIG BOOK OF CRICKET RULES

AND IT SAYS IN HERE THAT YOU HAVE TO ROLL THE PITCH, WE'LL TAKE CARE OF THAT FOR YOU.

CRUNCH!

KEEP GOING.

THANKS, UNCLE RAB.

NAE TROUBLE, LADDIE.

LOOK WHAT THEY'VE DONE TO WOR HAMPER. THEY'VE SQUISHED IT.

YOU'VE FLATTENED OUR SANDWICHES.

AYE, YOUR FIZZY JUICE HAS GONE FLAT, TOO.

WATCH WHAT YOU'RE DOING WITH THE WHITEWASH.

WE'RE JUST MARKING THE PITCH, AND YOU LOT AS WELL.

INTERNATIONAL TEST MATCHES ARE PLAYED IN WHITE KIT.

SPLOSH!

WE'LL HELP YOU WITH THAT - NO NEED TO THANK US.

THANK YOU? WE'LL MARMALISE YOU!

MARMALISING'S AGAINST THE RULES. NOW, I JUST HAVE TO PUT THE STUMPS INTO THE GROUND.

NOT ON ME FOOT!

IS THAT LEG BEFORE WICKET?

I'LL SHOW YOU LOT HOW CRICKET'S PLAYED.
I CAN HANDLE ANYTHING THIS BIG DRIP SENDS DOWN.
STEADY ON! THAT'S WAY TOO HIGH!
HOWZAT?
ERK!
AND YOU'RE OUT.
DINNA BE SILLY. THAT WAS A BAD BALL!
POOR BATSMEN ALWAYS BLAME THEIR TOOLS!
TIME FOR A PROPER TEST MATCH.
YOU'LL BE NO TEST FOR US.
OW!
TAKE THAT!
NO, THANKS. YOU ALREADY LET ME HAVE TWO!
YEOW!
GET OUT OF IT! ALL OF YOU.
WE'RE ALL OUT!
AYE, LACK OF BRAIN STOPPED PLAY.

DANDYTOWN SCOUTS! NEVER PREPARED!

George Harry Noah Olivia Emily Meera

WE'RE GOING TO MAKE A START ON OUR FARMING BADGE TODAY.

YAY!

LOOK AT THE LITTLE COW, IT'S SO COOL!

SHLUP!

I'M... COVERED... IN... COW... SPIT...

COME ON, WE'RE MEETING THE FARMER OVER HERE, HE'S GOING TO GIVE US SOME THINGS TO PLANT BACK AT THE SCOUT HALL.

WAIT... WHAT'S THAT...

...WHIFF?!

UGH!

ACK!

I HEAR YOU'RE PLANTING A CROP. I'LL GET YOU SOME SEEDS.

WE'RE EXCITED, HONESTLY, THIS IS THEIR EXCITED FACES.

DO I STILL HAVE A FACE? I THOUGHT THE STENCH BURNED IT OFF.

WHERE'S HARRY?

HERE I AM! LOOK WHAT I FOUND, ISN'T SHE BRILLIANT?

WHAT ABOUT THE STINK?

THE PIG WILL GET USED TO HIM, WE ALL HAVE.

BYE, PAL, I'VE GOT TO GO GET A BADGE.

SAD OINK!

IS THIS THE KIND OF CROPS YOU YOUNGSTERS WANT TO GROW?

YOUNGSTERS?

THEY'RE IN HERE. I THINK THEY'LL HAVE TO GROW SMALLER CROPS SO I CAN FIND THEM, THOUGH.

HI, MEERA, IS THERE A BADGE FOR HIDE AND SEEK?

REMEMBER TO PLOUGH YOUR FIELD FIRST THEN PLANT THE SEEDS, YOUNGSTERS.

THANKS! THAT'S THE FIRST OF THE BADGE DONE - RESEARCHING THE PLANTING.

WE ONLY HAVE TO PLANT THE SEEDS AND WE'LL GET A BADGE - FINALLY!

BACK AT THE SCOUT HUT...

I GOT THIS MINI-PLOUGH FROM A GADGET SHOP FOR OUR GARDEN AT HOME.

I KNEW YOU'D HAVE AN APP FOR THIS, NOAH!

DANDY TOWN SCOUTS

ON OFF

WEIRD, IT DID THAT AT HOME, TOO.

URRGH!

SPLUT!

IT'S DUG UP THE FIELD THOUGH.

AND WE CAN PLANT THE SEED.

SOMEONE HAS FOLLOWED THEM FROM THE FARM...

I CAN'T SEE MY NEW CHUM, HARRY BUT I'D HATE TO WASTE ALL THIS LOVELY MUD.

HOW LONG WILL IT TAKE SOMETHING TO GROW?

IT'LL TAKE AGES BEFORE WE GET ANYTHING.

SHOWS WHAT YOU KNOW...

...WE GREW A PIG!

WHAT? THAT'S NOT POSSIBLE!

I THOUGHT SHE'D RUN OFF THIS WAY. TIME TO GO BACK TO THE FARM.

SIGH... WE CAN FORGET ABOUT THAT BADGE.

DANDYTOWN'S GOT T★LENT!

WELCOME BACK TO DANDYTOWN'S GOT TALENT! OUR NEXT CONTESTANT IS... DESPERATE DAN!

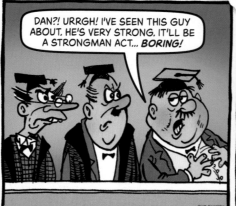

DAN?! URRGH! I'VE SEEN THIS GUY ABOUT. HE'S VERY STRONG. IT'LL BE A STRONGMAN ACT... *BORING!*

SO, DAN, WHAT WILL YOU BE DOING FOR US TONIGHT?

TONIGHT, KORKY, I'LL BE TRYING TO BREAK THE WORLD RECORD IN...

...PIE EATING!

GASP!

A GIANT PIE IS BROUGHT ON TO THE STAGE...

I WILL NOW EAT THIS ENTIRE PIE IN FIVE MINUTES!

NOT IF *I* EAT IT FIRST, YOU WON'T!

LAUNCH!

WHAT?!

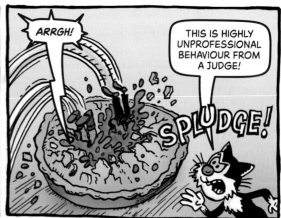

ARRGH!

THIS IS HIGHLY UNPROFESSIONAL BEHAVIOUR FROM A JUDGE!

SPLUDGE!

MURFLE BORP BLURG!*

SCOFF!

SCOFF!

*TRANSLATION - STOP EATING MY PIE!

FIVE MINUTES LATER...

DID I BREAK THE RECORD?

FOR HAVING A FIGHT IN A PIE?

NO.

WHAT'S FOR PUDDING?

DREADLOCK HOLMES

SLAM!

THAT WAS A GREAT BOOK! I LOVE MYSTERY NOVELS!

WAIT A MINUTE... WASN'T THERE A MYSTERY THAT I WAS MEANT TO BE SOLVING TODAY?

THAT'S WEIRD! I ALWAYS HAVE A MYSTERY TO SOLVE!

WHAT AM I FORGETTING? MAYBE MUM CAN HELP ME REMEMBER.

MUM, DO YOU HAVE ANY MYSTERIES FOR ME TO SOLVE?

YES, I DO AS IT HAPPENS!

THE MYSTERY OF WHETHER YOU WANT TOAST OR CEREAL FOR BREAKFAST!

THAT'S NOT A REAL MYSTERY!

CEREAL, PLEASE.

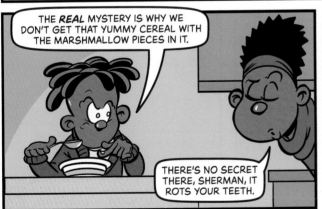

THE REAL MYSTERY IS WHY WE DON'T GET THAT YUMMY CEREAL WITH THE MARSHMALLOW PIECES IN IT.

THERE'S NO SECRET THERE, SHERMAN, IT ROTS YOUR TEETH.

WHY DON'T YOU GO AND BOTHER YOUR SISTER?

A MARSHA MYSTERY, MAYBE? GOOD IDEA!

MARSHA, DO YOU HAVE ANY MYSTERIES THAT NEED SOLVING?!

YES!

THE MYSTERY OF HOW SOMEONE AS BRILLIANT AS ME CAN BE RELATED TO SOMEONE LIKE YOU!

OH, HA-HA. VERY FUNNY, I DON'T THINK.

SO...

WHAT'S YOUR LATEST CASE, DREADLOCK?

THE MYSTERY OF THE MISSING MYSTERY!

ISN'T THAT JUST ANOTHER WAY OF SAYING YOU DON'T KNOW WHAT TO DO?

WOW!

NO! IT MEANS THAT THE MYSTERY COULD BE ANYWHERE!

WE COULD FIND OUR MYSTERY IN A HISTORY LESSON!

ALL OF HISTORY IS A MYSTERY TO ME!

HISTORY

IT COULD BE SOMEWHERE IN THIS LUNCH HALL!

THE REAL MYSTERY IS WHAT'S IN THESE SCHOOL DINNERS!

WE COULD EVEN FIND THE MYSTERY PLAYING FOOTBALL!

HERE'S A MYSTERY - WHY DON'T YOU PASS ME THE BALL WHEN I'M THE MUCH BETTER PLAYER?!

MAYBE THERE JUST WASN'T A MYSTERY TODAY!

OKAY, CLASS! TIME TO HAND IN YOUR MATHS HOMEWORK!

THAT WAS THE MYSTERY I WAS FORGETTING ABOUT! THE MYSTERY OF HOW TO SOLVE THE EQUATIONS IN MY MATHS HOMEWORK!

FIND THE ANGLE FOR X

DETENTION!

SHERMAN, YOU'RE A SMART BOY. WHY DO YOU KEEP ENDING UP IN DETENTION?

I DON'T KNOW. IT'S A MYSTERY!

PREVIOUSLY IN THIS ANNUAL...

WHAT ARE WE GOING TO DO? WE'RE THE WORLD'S STINKIEST TOWN!

LET'S MOVE TO THE MOON!

EVERYONE IN TOWN MOVED TO THE MOON IN A GIANT ROCKET AND NEW DANDYTOWN WAS BUILT ON THE SURFACE...

THE ROCKET USED TO GET TO THE MOON IS NOW THE TOWN HALL...

LET'S HAVE A PARTY TO CELEBRATE THE MOVE!

YEAH!

THE NEXT MORNING...

I'M STILL FULL! DID YOU TRY THOSE MOON PIES?

YEAH, THE MOON CAKES WERE BETTER, THOUGH.

THAT'S ALL THE RUBBISH FROM THE PARTY TIDIED.

LET'S EXPLORE!

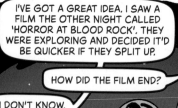

I'VE GOT A GREAT IDEA. I SAW A FILM THE OTHER NIGHT CALLED 'HORROR AT BLOOD ROCK'. THEY WERE EXPLORING AND DECIDED IT'D BE QUICKER IF THEY SPLIT UP.

HOW DID THE FILM END?

I DON'T KNOW. I WENT TO BED. BUT EVERYONE PROBABLY HAD A LOVELY TIME.

BECAUSE NOTHING COULD POSSIBLY GO WRONG WITH SPLITTING UP, THE TOWNSFOLK ALL SPLIT UP TO EXPLORE THE MOON...

LEAD THE WAY, OFFICER BOBBY.

THIS WAY, CLOTT. WE NEED TO ESTABLISH A MOON BASE.

YES, YOUR MAJESTY!

I'M WORRIED, BERYL.

ABOUT ALIENS? NO SUCH THING.

NO, ABOUT THE LACK OF KEYHOLES ON THE MOON.

INSTEAD OF LOOKING IN KEYHOLES, WHAT ABOUT THESE MOON HOLES?

THOSE AREN'T HOLES! THEY'RE CRATERS FORMED WHEN AN ASTEROID HITS.

LOOKS LIKE A HOLE TO ME.

WHOA!

LET'S SEE WHAT'S DOWN THERE.

WELL, THIS ISN'T SPOOKY AT ALL!

MEANWHILE, THE KID COPS HAVE FOUND...

AN ALIEN CITY!

SHINY!

ELSEWHERE...

BECAUSE NO-ONE EVER FOUND ANYTHING BAD ON A CRASHED ALIEN SPACESHIP!

WE COULD MAKE A BASE IN THIS OLD SPACESHIP.

WHILE BACK WITH BERYL AND KATE...

LOOK, CITY RUINS!

THERE'LL BE A MILLION KEYHOLES DOWN THERE!

MEANWHILE, THE CITY THE KID COPS FOUND IS VERY MUCH NOT RUINS...

SPARKLY!

IT'S SO CLEAN AND NEW, BUT WHERE IS EVERYONE?

COLONEL GRUMBLY AND CLOTT ARE EXPLORING THE ALIEN SHIP...

I KNOW YOU'RE SCARED, CLOTT, BUT I CAN'T CARRY YOU FOREVER!

IN THE UNDERGROUND RUINS...

COOL! THIS IS LIKE THOSE ANCIENT EGYPTIAN WRITINGS. YOU CAN SORT OF READ THEM LIKE A COMIC.

BORING! WHERE ARE THE KEYHOLES AT?

UNDERGROUND WITH KATE AND BERYL...

ARRGH!

THE KID COPS...

ARRGH!

ARRGH!

ARRGH TOO!

ARRGH AS WELL!

A TOWN MEETING IS CALLED...

I'VE DECIDED I DON'T LIKE THE MOON.

THAT GIANT EYEBALL ISN'T FRIENDLY AT ALL!

WHAT GIANT EYEBALL?! IT WAS A CHOMPY THING.

NO! IT WAS A ROBOT.

WHAT ARE YOU LOT GOING ON ABOUT? IT WAS *SPACE VAMPIRES!*

SPACE VAMPIRES?! IT WAS *MOON GHOSTS* FOR US.

EYEBALLS, CHOMPY THINGS, ROBOTS, VAMPIRES *AND* MOON GHOSTS?! THE MOON'S A BUSY PLACE.

THE MOON CAN'T HAVE *THAT* MANY MONSTERS.

DREADLOCK HOLMES GOES OUT TO MEET THE GIANT EYEBALL...

HMM... I WONDER...

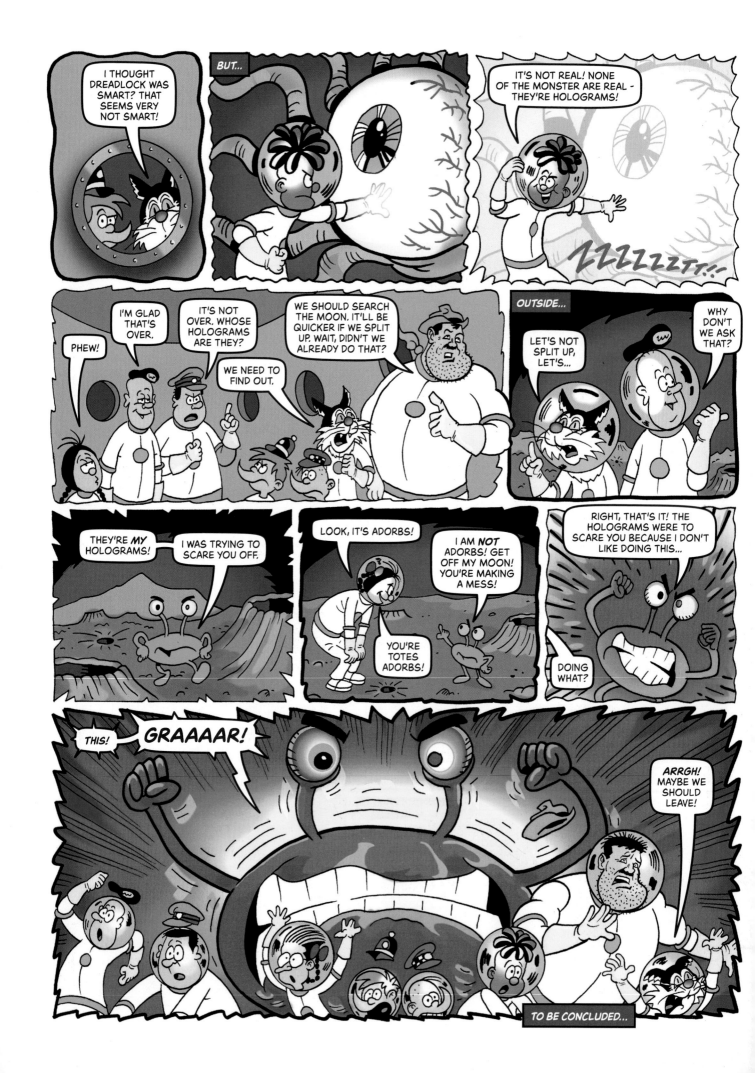

DANDYTOWN'S GOT T★LENT!

WELCOME BACK TO DANDYTOWN'S GOT TALENT! OUR NEXT CONTESTANT IS CORPORAL CLOTT!

AND WHAT WILL YOU BE DOING FOR US TONIGHT, CLOTT?

TONIGHT, KORKY, I'M GOING TO BE A TALENT SHOW JUDGE!

ER.... WHAT?

THE MEAN ONE, KORKY. THERE'S ALWAYS A MEAN ONE.

AREN'T YOU THE MEAN ONE?

ME?! I'M LOVELY!

YOU CAN ACTUALLY BE QUITE HURTFUL AT TIMES.

SO, WHAT ARE YOU GOING TO DO FOR US TODAY? COME ON! I'VE GOT A LOT OF ACTS TO GET THROUGH!

IS HE TALKING TO US? I'M CONFUSED. WHAT'S HAPPENING?

WE'RE THE JUDGES! YOU'RE THE ACT!

I'VE SEEN A LOT OF JUDGE ACTS IN MY TIME. WHAT MAKES YOU DIFFERENT?

WE... I, ER...

...

WE SING!

GO ON THEN!

SING?! SING WHAT?! WE NEED A SONG WE ALL KNOW FOR A START.

ER...

HAPPY BIRTHDAY TO YOU! HAPPY BIRTHDAY TO YOU!

IT'S MY BIRTHDAY! I FORGOT!

IT'S NOT HIS BIRTHDAY. - ED

HAPPY BIRTHDAY DEAR CLOTT.!!! HAPPY BIRTHDAY TO YOU!!

YOU'RE THE WINNERS!

HA-HA! WE WON! I WANT TO THANK MY PARENTS FOR BELIEVING IN ME.

NO, NO! STOP! YOU'VE WON NOTHING!

YOU'VE WON A MILLION POUNDS!

ARRGH! A MILLION POUNDS?! NOBODY'S WON ANYTHING! NEXT ACT! QUICK!

THE JOCKS AND THE GEORDIES

AND HERE, JUST ON THE RIGHT SIDE OF THE BORDER, IS A HAGGIS, OUT GRAZING IN THE WILD.

HUH?

THIS CHARMING, TIMID CREATURE AVOIDS CONTACT WI' HUMANS WHEN IT CAN.

ALTHOUGH THEY CAN BE TEMPTED OUT O' HIDING WITH CHOCOLATE OATY BISCUITS.

THIS IS A BRILLIANT NATURE DOCUMENTARY. WE'RE BOUND TO WIN THE FILMMAKING CONTEST.

AYE, WE ARE THAT!

SO THAT'S WHAT THEY'RE UP TO - A FILMMAKING CONTEST. WELL, THERE'S JUST ONE THING FOR US TO DO...

...RUIN THEIR FILM!

AND THE HAGGIS CONTINUE TO GRAZE...

AYE, AND WE'D ENJOY IT MORE WITHOUT THE COMMENTARY!

WHAT'S THAT?

IT LOOKS LIKE THE HAGGIS HAVE HEARD SOMETHING.

AND IT'S HOWAY THE LADS...

SQUONK!

SCATTER, LADS! RUN!

IT'S A HAGGIS STAMPEDE!

WE'VE BEEN HAGGISED. OUR FILM IS RUINED.

WAS THAT US? WE'RE REET SORRY AN' THAT.

AYE, REET SORRY WE DIDN'T GET IT ON FILM!

BACK AT THEIR HUT...

THE BEST WAY TO ANNOY THE JOCKS WOULD BE TO WIN THE FILMMAKING CONTEST. WE JUST NEED TO THINK OF AN IDEA TO MAKE A FILM ABOUT.

SHOULD BE EASY.

AYE, SHOULD BE. WE'LL THINK OF SOMETHING SOON.

HOURS AND HOURS AND HOURS LATER...

SOMETHING'S BOUND TO HIT US SOON.

CRASH!

EEK!

OUCH!

ARRGH!

THAT'S IT! WE'LL MAKE A FILM ABOUT FOOTBALL.

CHAMPION!

THE NEXT MORNING...

WE'VE GOT EVERYTHING WE NEED FOR FOOTBALL IN THIS HAMPER.

JUST LIKE PROFESSIONAL TEAMS DO.

BUT...

BUGS!

MOTHS!

AND THEY WERE HUNGRY MOTHS AS WELL.

WE'LL HAVE TO USE THE OLDER KITS.

THESE ARE PROPER OLD KITS, MIND.

THEY EVEN COME WITH MOUSTACHES.

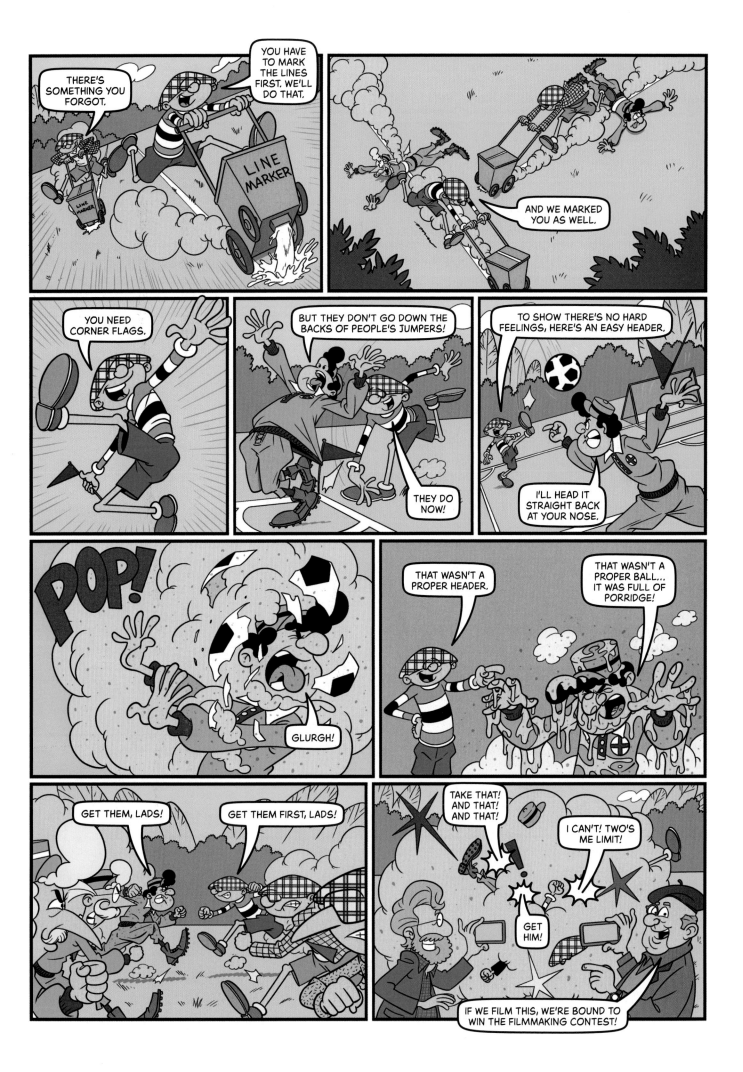

GEORGE vs DRAGON

SWEETIE VILLE

KANE VILLE

LAYLA VILLE

HYDRA

CERBERUS

TIM

MY MUM'S A... SUPER VILLAIN

Panel 1:

PLAYING A GAME, ARE YOU? GAMES SEEM POPULAR WITH CHILDREN THESE DAYS.

YES, MUM, EVERYONE LOVES THEM.

PEW! PEW!

Panel 2:

DO THEY NOW? MWAH-HA-HA!

HA-HA-HA!

HA-HA-HA!

Panel 3:

HA-HA-HA!

HA-HA-HA!

HA-HA-HA!

HA-HA-HA!

HA-HA-HA!

THAT'S MUM'S 'I'VE THOUGHT OF AN EVIL PLAN' LAUGH. IT GOES ON A BIT.

HUSBAND! EVERY KID LIKES PLAYING GAMES.

AND?

I'VE BEEN CODING ALL MORNING TO CREATE THE WORLD'S MOST ENTERTAINING GAME!

HOW DOES THAT HELP US TAKE OVER THE WORLD?

HIDDEN IN THE CODE IS A HYPNOTIC COMMAND! ANYONE WHO PLAYS THIS GAME WILL BE UNDER OUR CONTROL!

A WORLDWIDE ARMY OF KIDS! I LIKE IT!

SWEETIE IS LISTENING IN...

MWAH-HA-HA!

MUM TAKES A BREAK FOR LUNCH, SO SWEETIE SNEAKS IN TO GET ON THE COMPUTER...

LET'S SEE IF THIS GAME CAN REALLY TAKE OVER YOUR...

...MIIIIIIND!

WHOA! I JUST LOOKED AT IT FOR A SECOND! THIS IS DANGEROUS.

I NEED TO HACK THE CODE OF THIS GAME AND REWRITE IT SO IT'S HARMLESS.

ER...

George · Harry · Noah · Olivia · Emily · Meera

DANDYTOWN SCOUTS!

NEVER PREPARED!

IT'S FRIDAY EVENING, WHICH MEANS THE DANDYTOWN SCOUTS MEET...

GOOD EVENING, SCOUTS! IS EVERYBODY READY TO START TRYING FOR A BADGE? *AGAIN!*

CAN WE GET OUR ASTRONAUT BADGE?

I DON'T THINK THERE IS AN ASTRONAUT BADGE - UNLESS YOU WORK FOR NASA.

THAT'S A BIT RUBBISH. I REALLY WANT TO BE AN ASTRONAUT.

WHO LIKES COOKING?

WE DO!

WELL... WE LIKE *EATING!*

THAT'S A START, I SUPPOSE. NOW, WHAT WILL WE COOK?

CHIPS!

CHOCOLATE!

CHOCOLATE *AND* CHIPS!

AND CAKE!

WE SHOULD HAVE A *HEALTHY* MENU IF WE WANT OUR BADGE.

THAT'S RIGHT, EMILY.

YEAH, I WAS JUST GOING TO SAY THAT, BEING *LEADER* AND ALL.

SO...

SHOPPING FOR INGREDIENTS IS PART OF GETTING THE BADGE, SO EVERYBODY BE CAREFUL IN HERE.

BEANS HALF PRICE

I'VE GOT A TROLLEY! MUM NEVER LETS ME PUSH ONE!

ZOOM!

WATCH OUT, HARRY! YOU'RE HEADING STRAIGHT FOR...

HEH-HEH... SORRY ABOUT THAT! I CAN SEE WHAT MUM MEANS NOW!

GRR!

CRASH!

DANDYTOWN'S GOT TALENT!

WELCOME BACK TO DANDYTOWN'S GOT TALENT. OUR NEXT CONTESTANTS ARE CUDDLES AND DIMPLES!

AND WHAT WILL YOU BE DOING FOR US TONIGHT, CUDDLES AND DIMPLES?

TONIGHT, KORKY, WE'LL BE JUGGLING.

BERYL THE PERIL'S DONE JUGGLING ALREADY!

WITH CHAINSAWS?!

STOP! WE'VE ALREADY SEEN THIS! YOU SAY 'CHAINSAWS' AND THEN YOUR PARENTS COME ON AND STOP YOU.

BUT...

THEY'RE BABIES! AREN'T THEIR PARENTS GOING TO STOP THEM?!

3...2...1...

BRRR BRRR

MEANWHILE...

CUDDLES AND DIMPLES ARE QUIET.

IT'S THEIR NAP TIME, THEY'RE ASLEEP.

WELL, IN THAT CASE...

...I'M HAVING A NAP TOO!

BACK AT THE TALENT SHOW...

OH! THE CHAINSAWS ARE ON FIRE NOW!

EEEK!

NOTE FROM THE EDITOR...

WARNING! DO NOT ATTEMPT TO JUGGLE FLAMING CHAINSAWS AT HOME. JUGGLING FLAMING CHAINSAWS IS DANGEROUS AND SHOULD ONLY BE ATTEMPTED BY HIGHLY TRAINED BABIES!

CUDDLES AND DIMPLES FINISH THEIR ACT...

TA-DA!

WHERE'D THEY GO?

OUTSIDE...

STUDIO

DO YOU THINK IT'S SAFE TO GO BACK IN?

DREADLOCK HOLMES

AHA! SO THAT'S WHERE MY LUCKY HAT WAS...

...IN MY SISTER'S ROOM!

ANOTHER MYSTERY SOLVED BY DREADLOCK HOLMES, THE WORLD'S GREATEST DETECTIVE.

I AM SO GOOD AT SOLVING MYSTERIES THAT IT REALLY ISN'T FAIR TO ANYONE ELSE.

I SHOULD LET OTHER PEOPLE BE DETECTIVES.

I GIVE YOU...

...THE MYSTERY OF THE MISSING DETECTIVE! IS ANYONE SMART ENOUGH TO FIND ME?

A LOT LATER...

HMPH

I THOUGHT SOMEONE WOULD'VE FOUND ME BY NOW.

LATER STILL...

I LOVE THIS TV SHOW!

SHH! THIS IS THE GOOD BIT!

HOW CAN THEY NOT KNOW I'M UNDER THE CUSHIONS THEY'RE SITTING ON?

MAYBE I MADE THIS MYSTERY TOO HARD FOR THEM. I KNOW WHAT TO DO.

SO, DREADLOCK TRIES AGAIN...

THIS SHOULD MAKE THINGS A LITTLE EASIER!

Where is Dreadlock? It's a mystery! Is this a clue?

WHEREVER COULD SHERMAN BE?

I DON'T KNOW, IT'S A MYSTERY!

Where is Dreadlock? It's a mystery! Is this a clue?

HEE-HEE!

IF SHERMAN WAS HERE, THEN HE WOULD PROBABLY WANT THESE BISCUITS.

BUT HE ISN'T, SO I'LL EAT THEM ALL.

NO!

Where is Dreadlock? It's a mystery! Is this a clue?

IF SHERMAN WAS HERE WE COULD WATCH HIS FAVOURITE DETECTIVE SHOW, BUT HE ISN'T, SO I'LL WATCH MY SOAPS INSTEAD!

NO!

Where is Dreadlock? It's a mystery! Is this a clue?

YES, IT'S SUCH A SHAME SHERMAN IS MISSING OUT.

HEE-HEE!

THIS ISN'T WORKING. MY FAMILY JUST AREN'T SMART ENOUGH TO FIND ME.

MAYBE SOMEONE AT SCHOOL TOMORROW WILL BE A PROPER DETECTIVE.

THE NEXT DAY...

I WONDER IF ANYONE WILL BE ABLE TO FIND ME AT SCHOOL.

SAM?

HERE!

SHERMAN?

SHERMAN?

OH NO! IF I SAY THAT I'M HERE, THEN PEOPLE WILL KNOW WHERE I AM! WHAT DO I DO?

SHERMAN? IF YOU'RE HERE, THEN YOU HAVE TO SAY SO!

I'LL GIVE THEM A CLUE. A TRUE DETECTIVE WILL WORK OUT THAT I'M HERE!

HERE!

I SUPPOSE THAT'S GOOD ENOUGH.

LATER...

I'VE BEEN HIDING IN DIFFERENT PLACES ALL DAY AND NO-ONE HAS FOUND ME!

THUNK!

THAT DOESN'T COUNT.

LATER STILL...

LIBRARY

MAYBE I'VE BEEN MAKING THIS TOO HARD, NOT EVERYONE IS AS BRILLIANT AS ME.

I'LL GIVE PEOPLE SOME CLUES ABOUT WHERE I AM.

ATTENTION! THERE IS A CLUE...

EXCUSE ME, YOUNG MAN...

... IF YOU WANT TO PLAY GAMES THEN I SUGGEST YOU USE THE PLAYGROUND!

AT HOME TIME...

NOBODY FOUND ME ALL DAY!

MAYBE NO-ONE IS AS GOOD A DETECTIVE AS I AM. YES, THAT'S PROBABLY IT.

MUM! I'M HOME!

SHERMAN! WHERE ARE YOU? IT'S TIME FOR YOU TO DO YOUR CHORES AND TIDY YOUR ROOM!

MAYBE THERE ARE SOME GOOD THINGS ABOUT NOBODY BEING ABLE TO FIND YOU!

OH, SO NOW HE'S GOOD AT HIDING! TYPICAL!

DANDYTOWN'S GOT T★LENT!

ARRGH! BACK TO EARTH! BACK TO EARTH!

INSIDE THE SPACESHIP...

IT WON'T START! WHY WON'T IT START?

IT RUNS ON BUM GAS, AND WE'RE ALL OUT!

HANG ON, DON'T WE ALL HAVE BUMS?

QUICK! EVERYONE NEEDS TO FILL THEIR SPACE TROUSERS WITH BOTTOM BURPS!

BUTT... I MEAN, BUT...

IT'S WEIRD, WHEN YOU'RE AT A WEDDING YOU CAN'T KEEP IT IN, BUT WHEN YOU ACTUALLY NEED TO LET RIP - NOTHING!

WAIT! I'VE GOT SOMETHING!

I'M GOING TO *LET RIP* RIGHT ABOUT NOW!

PARP!

THAT WOULDN'T GET A MOUSE'S CAR ACROSS A LIVING ROOM!

ER... GUYS! THE THING IS RIGHT OUTSIDE!

AND IT DOESN'T SEEM HAPPY!

GRR! I'M NOT HAPPY!

DAN TELLS EVERYONE HIS PLAN...

SO...

IT'S DECIDED THAT POSTMAN PRAT HAS THE FASTEST LEGS...

MEANWHILE...

AND...

DAN TAKES A RUN UP, AND...

...THROWS THE SHIP INTO SPACE!

HE SAVED US BUT HAD TO STAY BEHIND!

WHAT A HERO!

ON THE MOON...

FADE DISAPPEAR!

THE BIG ALIEN WAS JUST ANOTHER HOLOGRAM! - ED

GOOD RIDDANCE!

WHERE'S DAN? - ED

THE Dandy

NEE-NAW NEE-NAW NEE-NAW!